Salads & Sides

**Recipes Featured on TV
by Meriel Bradley**

Salads & Sides

Website: www.MerielBradley.com

Copyright © 2002 by Emmadee Communications Inc.

Published by EXI International Inc.

Forward

SALADS & SIDES is the natural complement to my book "INDOOR GRILLING". Now you can add delicious salads and side dishes to any meal quickly and easily.

I've designed the recipes to be easy to follow, simple to prepare, and delicious to eat - all to help you add a little extra flare to you meals without spending hours in the kitchen.

Featuring fresh, pure ingredients, these homegrown recipes will be a pleasure to prepare and will surely become family favorites.

Follow the Quick Tips and learn how to maximize your time in the kitchen, enhance your meals and bring the best to your table and family.

SALADS & SIDES will help you round out your meals with a whole new world of food. Enjoy!

Meriel Bradley

Salads & Sides

Website: www.MerielBradley.com

VISIT WWW.MERIELBRADLEY.COM TO:

- Send your comments
- Submit recipes, tips and ideas for inclusion in upcoming books and on TV
- Preview future volumes in the Meriel Bradley cookbook series

NOTES ON COOKING TIMES

Cooking times given are approximate only. Please follow the directions given in the instruction manual for your own model and make of appliance.

A meat or food thermometer can be used to measure the internal temperature of meats and ensure your food is properly cooked.

Contents

Salads

My Favorite Mixed Salad

1 romaine heart chopped
$^1/_2$ English cucumber diced
1 cup baby spinach
$^1/_2$ cup sliced mushrooms
$^1/_2$ cup whole cherry tomatoes
$^1/_2$ cup baby corn chopped

1 Wash all salad ingredients well and dry before chopping.

2 Place all the ingredients in a salad bowl and toss with your favorite dressing. See recipes on pages 28 to 32.

3 Refrigerate until ready to serve.

QUICK TIP

If a salad is lacking in flavor, it could be because it was not dried well after washing. Try using a salad spinner to help ensure your salad is properly dried.

Serves: 2 - 3

Preparation time: 10 minutes

Cucumber Salad

³/₄ English cucumber
3 tablespoons natural yogurt
1 clove garlic crushed to a
    paste with ¹/₄ teaspoon
    salt
Fresh ground pepper to taste

1 Wash the cucumber well and dry before grating.

2 Grate the cucumber and squeeze by the handful to remove any excess water.

3 Place in a bowl and stir in all the remaining ingredients.

4 Refrigerate until ready to serve.

Serves: 3 - 4

Preparation time: 10 minutes

Apple & Walnut Salad

3 apples (your favorite) cubed
1/2 cup walnut pieces
1/2 cup raisins
1/2 cup mayonnaise
Fresh ground salt to taste

1 Wash the apples well and dry before chopping.

2 Mix all the ingredients in a bowl.

3 Refrigerate until ready to serve, but this is better served straight away.

Serves: 3 - 4

Preparation time: 10 minutes

Coleslaw

2 cups finely shredded white
  cabbage
1 cup finely shredded purple
  cabbage
1 cup grated carrot
$\frac{1}{2}$ cup mayonnaise
$\frac{1}{2}$ tablespoon white vinegar
Fresh ground salt to taste

1. Wash all salad ingredients well and dry before chopping.

2. Place the shredded cabbage and carrots in a bowl.

3. Mix the remaining ingredients together, pour over the cabbage, and mix well.

4. Refrigerate until ready to serve.

QUICK TIP

Serving sizes will depend on the number of other dishes prepared for the meal.

Serves: 3 - 4

Preparation time: 15 minutes

Tomato Salad

4 ripe tomatoes
1 scallion chopped
2 tablespoons chopped fresh
    chives
2 tablespoons balsamic
    vinegar
$1/4$ teaspoon paprika
Fresh ground salt to taste

1 Wash all salad ingredients well and dry before chopping.

2 Slice the tomatoes and arrange in a flat open dish.

3 Sprinkle with the remaining ingredients.

4 Refrigerate until ready to serve.

Serves: 3 - 4

Preparation time: 5 minutes

Salads & Sides by Meriel Bradley :: *www.MerielBradley.com*

Sliced Carrot Salad

3 cups sliced carrots - cooked
1 green pepper cut into strips
1 cup red Spanish onion diced
1 can tomato soup
1 cup sugar
½ cup vinegar
½ cup cooking oil
1 teaspoon Worcestershire
   sauce
1 teaspoon dry mustard
Fresh ground salt to taste

1 Wash all salad ingredients well and dry before chopping.

2 Combine all the ingredients together.

3 Refrigerate until ready to serve.

4 Before serving, remove the vegetables from the sauce with a slotted spoon.

Serves: 4 - 5

Preparation time: 15 minutes

Potato Salad

2 cups yellow flesh potatoes
    peeled and diced 1 inch
    square
$^1/_2$ cup mayonnaise
4 tablespoons chopped fresh
    parsley
Paprika to garnish

1 Wash all salad ingredients well and dry before chopping.

2 Steam or boil the potatoes for 10 - 15 minutes or until soft.

3 Allow to cool.

4 Place in a bowl and carefully mix in the parsley and mayonnaise.

5 Sprinkle the top with paprika.

6 Refrigerate until ready to serve.

> **QUICK TIP**
> *When using fresh herbs chop the leaves finely to release the flavor.*

Serves: 3 - 4

Preparation time: 10 minutes

Salads & Sides by Meriel Bradley :: www.MerielBradley.com

Bean Salad

1 cup cooked white kidney beans
1 cup cooked red kidney beans
1 cup corn
2 tablespoons chopped fresh chives
2 tablespoons olive oil
1 tablespoon balsamic vinegar
Fresh ground salt and pepper to taste

1 Wash all salad ingredients well and dry before chopping.

2 Mix all the ingredients together.

3 Refrigerate until ready to serve.

Serves: 2 - 3

Preparation time: 10 minutes

Pasta & Egg Salad

2 cups cooked pasta
2 hard boiled eggs chopped
1 cup baby corn chopped
1 cup corn
1 cup cucumber chopped
1 cup mushrooms chopped
3 dill pickles chopped
$^1/_3$ cup Italian dressing
Croutons to serve

1. Wash all salad ingredients well and dry before chopping.

2. Mix all the ingredients together.

3. Refrigerate until ready to serve, and top with croutons.

Serves: 2 - 3

Preparation time: 10 minutes

Salads & Sides by Meriel Bradley :: www.MerielBradley.com

Mixed Salad

2 cups lettuce shredded
2 cups mixed salad greens
$\frac{1}{2}$ English cucumber diced
1 cup sprouts (your favorite
    type)
$\frac{1}{2}$ cup toasted sunflower
    seeds

1 Wash all salad ingredients well and dry before chopping.

2 Mix all the ingredients except the sunflower seeds and sprouts together.

3 Toss with your favorite dressing.

4 Refrigerate until ready to serve and then top with the sprouts and sunflower seeds.

Serves: 2 - 3

Preparation time: 10 minutes

Summer Salad

1 can tuna drained
1 cup whole cherry tomatoes
½ English cucumber diced
2 scallions chopped
1½ cups cooked new
    potatoes cut into small
    bite sized pieces
⅓ cup black olives chopped
2 tablespoons chopped fresh
    parsley
2 hard boiled eggs sliced

QUICK TIP

After chopping parsley try squeezing it dry in a small towel to remove all the excess water. You will get more flavor and it will last longer in the fridge.

1   Wash all salad ingredients well and dry before chopping.

2   Mix all the ingredients except the eggs together.

3   Toss with one recipe of Lemony Dressing (page 29) or your own store bought dressing.

4   Top with the sliced eggs.

5   Refrigerate until ready to serve.

Serves: 2 - 3

Preparation time: 10 minutes

Pasta & Salmon

2 cups cooked pasta
1 tin salmon
1 cup baby corn chopped
2 scallions chopped
1/3 cup mayonnaise

1. Wash the scallions well and dry before chopping.

2. Mix all the ingredients together.

3. Refrigerate until ready to serve.

Serves: 2 - 3

Preparation time: 10 minutes

Grilled Vegetable & Pasta Salad

2 cups cooked pasta
1 red pepper cut into strips
1 yellow pepper cut into strips
1 zucchini cut into strips
$\frac{1}{2}$ red onion sliced
1 tablespoon olive oil
1 teaspoon dried oregano
1 teaspoon dried parsley

1 Wash all salad ingredients well and dry before chopping.

2 Mix the peppers, zucchini and onion together with the olive oil and herbs.

3 If you have an electric grill, grill until just turning soft.

4 If you do not have an electric grill, place in a pan and saute until just turning soft.

5 Allow to cool and mix in the cooked pasta.

6 Add $\frac{1}{2}$ a recipe of Herb Dressing (page 28) or use your favorite store bought dressing.

7 Refrigerate until ready to serve.

QUICK TIP

If you prefer to use fresh herbs instead of dried herbs, use triple the amount of fresh herbs in place of the dried herb quantity.

Serves: 2 - 3

Preparation time: 10 minutes

Salads & Sides by Meriel Bradley :: www.MerielBradley.com

Shrimp Cocktail Salad

3 cups shredded lettuce
1 cup chopped cucumber
2 cups salad shrimp
$1/3$ cup mayonnaise
1 tablespoon lemon juice
1 tablespoon tomato paste
Fresh ground pepper to taste

1. Wash all salad ingredients well and dry before chopping.

2. Place the lettuce and cucumber into a bowl.

3. Mix remaining ingredients together and pile on top of the lettuce and cucumber.

4. Refrigerate until ready to serve.

Serves: 2 - 4

Preparation time: 10 minutes

Lettuce Roll-ups

1 large avocado
1 tablespoon plain natural
    yogurt
1 small clove garlic - crushed
Zest (or finely grated peel)
    $\frac{1}{2}$ lime
Juice $\frac{1}{2}$ lime
$\frac{1}{2}$ teaspoon French mustard
$\frac{1}{2}$ tomato finely diced
$\frac{1}{2}$ English cucumber finely
    diced
1 head romaine lettuce leaves
Fresh ground salt and pepper
    to taste

QUICK TIP

*If you don't have a zester,
you can use a fine grater for
the zest (the thin outer peel
of a citrus fruit) called for in
some recipes.*

1. Wash all salad ingredients well and dry before chopping.

2. Cut the avocado in half, remove the stone and scoop out the insides.

3. Mash together with the yogurt, garlic, lime zest and juice and mustard.

4. Mix in the tomatoes and cucumber and season well.

5. Pile onto the lettuce leaves, roll up and enjoy.

6. Refrigerate if not ready to serve, but this is best eaten straight away.

7. This is also great in a sandwich or as a dip.

Serves: 2 - 3

Preparation time: 15 minutes

Salads & Sides by Meriel Bradley :: www.MerielBradley.com

Egg Salad

8 hard boiled eggs peeled
   and quartered
$1/4$ cup purple onion chopped
$1/3$ cup mayonnaise
2 tablespoons chopped
   fresh dill
2 tablespoons chopped fresh
   parsley
1 tablespoon Dijon mustard
Paprika to garnish

1 Wash all salad ingredients well and dry before chopping.

2 Mix all the ingredients together.

3 Refrigerate until ready to serve.

Serves: 2 - 3

Preparation time: 10 minutes

Shrimp & Rice Salad

1 tablespoon butter
½ purple onion diced
1 clove garlic chopped
½ cup raisins
2 cups cooked rice
1 cup salad shrimp
1 cup canned corn

1. Melt the butter in a small pan and add the onion and garlic.

2. Cook until soft.

3. Stir in the raisins and allow to cool.

4. Transfer the onion and raisin mix to a bowl and stir in the remaining ingredients.

5. Refrigerate until ready to serve.

Serves: 2

Preparation time: 15 minutes

Salads & Sides by Meriel Bradley :: www.MerielBradley.com

Rice & Tuna Salad

2 cups cooked rice
1 can tuna drained
1 red pepper chopped
1 cup cooked peas

1 Wash the red pepper well and dry before chopping.

2 Mix all the ingredients together.

3 Toss with one $\frac{1}{2}$ recipe of Herb Dressing (page 28) or your favorite store bought dressing.

4 Refrigerate until ready to serve.

Serves: 2 - 3

Preparation time: 10 minutes

Rice & Mushroom Salad

2 cups cooked rice
1 green pepper finely diced
1 cup mushrooms finely diced

1. Wash all salad ingredients well and dry before chopping.

2. Mix all the ingredients together.

3. Toss with one $1/2$ recipe of Lemony Dressing (page 29) or your favorite store bought dressing.

4. Refrigerate until ready to serve.

Serves: 2 - 3

Preparation time: 10 minutes

Dressings

Herb Dressing

¹/₂ teaspoon fresh ground salt
1 clove garlic
2 tablespoons balsamic vinegar
4 tablespoons Greek olive oil
1 teaspoon chopped fresh
chives
1 teaspoon chopped fresh
parsley
1 teaspoon chopped fresh
oregano
Fresh ground pepper to taste

1 Wash all the herbs well and dry before chopping.

2 Crush the garlic to a paste with the salt.

3 Whisk in all the other ingredients.

4 Serve with your favorite salad.

QUICK TIP

Chives have a mild onion flavor. The pretty purple flowers make a unique garnish.

Preparation time: 10 minutes

Lemony Dressing

½ teaspoon fresh ground salt
1 clove garlic
3 tablespoons Greek olive oil
1 tablespoon lemon juice
2 teaspoons fresh chopped
 oregano
Fresh ground pepper to taste

1 Wash the oregano well and dry before chopping.

2 Crush the garlic to a paste with the salt.

3 Whisk in all the other ingredients.

4 Serve with your favorite salad.

Preparation time: 10 minutes

Sherry Dressing

4 tablespoons sweet sherry
3 tablespoons Greek olive oil
3 tablespoons white wine
   vinegar
1 teaspoon lemon juice
1 teaspoon fresh chopped
   thyme
Fresh ground salt and pepper
   to taste

1 Wash fresh thyme well and dry before chopping.

2 Whisk all the ingredients together.

3 Serve with your favorite salad.

Preparation time: 10 minutes

French Lemon & Herb Dressing

1/3 cup mayonnaise
3 tablespoons Greek olive oil
1 teaspoon sesame oil
Zest (or finely grated rind)
    1 lemon
Juice 1 lemon
1/3 cup parsley
1 clove garlic
1/4 teaspoon salt
1/2 teaspoon French mustard
Fresh ground pepper to taste

1 Wash the parsley & lemon well and dry before use.

2 Put all ingredients in a food processor or blender and grind to a smooth consistency.

3 Serve with your favorite salad.

Preparation time: 10 minutes

Balsamic Vinaigrette

¼ teaspoon salt
1 clove garlic
4 tablespoons balsamic vinegar
4 tablespoons Greek olive oil
Fresh ground pepper to taste

1 Crush the garlic to a paste with the salt.

2 Whisk in all the other ingredients.

3 Serve with your favorite salad.

QUICK TIP
*Use a small hand whisk
to mix dressing ingredients
together.*

Preparation time: 5 minutes

Salads & Sides by Meriel Bradley :: *www.MerielBradley.com*

Potatoes

Scalloped Potatoes

1 ½ pounds potatoes
2 tablespoons butter
1 tablespoon cornstarch
1 ½ cups milk
1 small can condensed
    mushroom soup
Fresh ground pepper to taste

1 Wash the potatoes well before chopping.

2 Slice the potatoes very thinly and arrange in a baking dish. Season with fresh ground pepper to taste.

3 Pre-heat the oven to 375 degrees F.

4 In a pan melt the butter and stir in the cornstarch to make a paste.

5 Add the milk a little at a time, stirring constantly.

6 Add the can of soup and mix to a smooth consistency.

7 Pour over the potatoes.

8 Place the dish in the oven and cook for 1 ½ hours or until the potatoes are tender.

Serves: 4

Preparation time: 20 minutes

Salads & Sides by Meriel Bradley :: *www.MerielBradley.com*

Mashed Potatoes

2 pounds potatoes peeled
   (Yukon gold or yellow flesh
   potatoes have great flavor)
2 tablespoons butter
Milk for mixing
Fresh ground salt and pepper
   to taste

1. Wash the potatoes well before chopping.

2. Cut potatoes into pieces and steam or boil until soft.

3. Add the butter and seasonings and mash with a potato masher.

4. Add enough milk to obtain a creamy consistency, and continue mashing until no lumps remain.

Serves: 4

Preparation time: 15 minutes

Mashed Potatoes with Onion

2 pounds potatoes peeled
   (Yukon gold or yellow flesh
   potatoes have great flavor)
1 cup onion diced
4 tablespoons butter
Milk for mixing
Fresh ground salt and pepper
   to taste

1 Wash the potatoes well before chopping.

2 Cut potatoes into pieces and steam or boil until soft.

3 Place 1 tablespoon of the butter into a pan and add the onion.

4 Saute until soft and golden.

5 Place the cooked potatoes in a bowl, add the remaining butter and seasonings and mash with a potato masher.

6 Add enough milk to obtain a creamy consistency, and continue mashing until no lumps remain.

7 Stir in the onions and serve.

Serves: 4

Preparation time: 15 minutes

Salads & Sides by Meriel Bradley :: www.MerielBradley.com

Roasted Parisian Potatoes

2 pounds Parisian potatoes
4 tablespoons melted butter
4 tablespoon olive oil
1 teaspoon paprika
$^1/_2$ teaspoon celery salt
Fresh ground salt and pepper
    to taste

1. Wash the potatoes well.

2. Pre-heat the oven to 375 degrees F.

3. Place the potatoes in a bowl and cover with hot tap water. Leave for 5 minutes, then drain and towel dry the potatoes.

4. Place the potatoes back into a dry bowl and add all the other ingredients.

5. Mix well. Place the potatoes onto a baking tray and pour over the excess butter, oil and seasonings.

6. Cook for 40 - 50 minutes or until the potatoes are soft, turning them once or twice during the cooking process.

Serves: 4

Preparation time: 10 minutes

Chipped Potatoes

1 pound Yukon Gold potatoes
  sliced very thinly into
  rounds
4 tablespoons melted butter
4 tablespoons olive oil
Fresh ground salt and pepper
  to taste

1 Wash the potatoes well before chopping.

2 Pre-heat the oven to 400 degrees F.

3 Place potatoes in a bowl and cover with hot water. Leave for 5 minutes then drain and towel dry the potatoes very well.

4 Mix the oil and butter together in a bowl.

5 Dip each potato slice into the oil and butter mix and place the potatoes onto a rack over a baking tray in one layer.

6 Season very well with the salt and pepper on each side.

7 Cook for 20 minutes until the potatoes are crisp, carefully turning them once or twice during the cooking process.

Serves: 4

Preparation time: 10 minutes

> **QUICK TIP**
>
> *To achieve a crisp finish, make sure your potatoes are nice and dry before adding the butter and oils.*

Potato Balls

2 pounds potatoes peeled
   (Yukon gold or yellow flesh
   potatoes have great flavor)
2 tablespoons butter
2 cups crushed soda crackers
1 medium onion finely diced
1 egg beaten
Milk for mixing
Fresh ground salt and pepper
   to taste

1   Wash the potatoes well before chopping.

2   Cut the potatoes into pieces and steam or boil until soft.

3   Add the butter and seasonings and mash with a potato masher.

4   Add enough milk to obtain a creamy consistency, and continue mashing until no lumps remain.

5   Stir in the onion and allow to cool.

6   Pre-heat the oven to 375 degrees F.

7   Mix in the egg.

8   Using your hands, form the mashed potato into 2 inch diameter balls and roll in the cracker crumbs to coat.

9   Place the balls on a baking tray and cook for 50 - 60 minutes.

Serves: 4 - 6

Preparation time: 15 minutes

Potato Balls with Cheese

2 pounds potatoes peeled
(Yukon gold or yellow flesh
potatoes have great flavor)
2 tablespoons butter
1 medium onion finely diced
2 cups crushed soda crackers
1 cup grated cheddar cheese
1 egg beaten
Milk for mixing
Fresh ground salt and pepper
to taste

1. Wash the potatoes well before chopping.

2. Cut the potatoes into pieces and steam or boil until soft.

3. Add the butter and seasonings and mash with a potato masher.

4. Add enough milk to obtain a creamy consistency, and continue mashing until no lumps remain.

5. Stir in the onion and allow to cool.

6. Pre-heat the oven to 375 degrees F.

7. Mix in the egg and cheese.

8. Using your hands, form the mashed potato into 2 inch diameter balls and roll in the cracker crumbs to coat.

9. Place the balls on a baking tray and cook for 50 - 60 minutes.

Serves: 4 - 6

Preparation time: 15 minutes

Salads & Sides by Meriel Bradley :: www.MerielBradley.com

Potatoes in Foil with Herbs

1 pound Yukon Gold potatoes diced 1 inch square
1/2 cup chopped fresh parsley
1 teaspoon dried thyme
1 teaspoon dried oregano
1 teaspoon dried Italian seasoning
4 tablespoons butter melted
Fresh ground salt and pepper to taste

1 Wash all vegetable ingredients well before chopping.

2 Pre-heat the oven to 375 degrees F.

3 Lay the potatoes on a large piece of foil and sprinkle over the herbs.

4 Pour over the butter and season well.

5 Fold the foil over to make a well sealed parcel.

6 Place the package on a baking sheet and place in the oven for 30 minutes or until the potatoes are soft.

QUICK TIP

Thyme has a very subtle, aromatic flavor and is a great herb to use in or alongside fish dishes.

Serves: 4

Preparation time: 15 minutes

Potatoes in Foil with Garlic & Onions

1 pound Yukon Gold potatoes
diced 1 inch square
1 cup red Spanish onion diced
½ cup chopped fresh parsley
4 tablespoons butter melted
with 1 clove of crushed
garlic
Fresh ground salt and pepper
to taste

1 Wash all vegetable ingredients well before chopping.

2 Pre-heat the oven to 375 degrees F.

3 Lay the potatoes and onions on a large piece of foil and sprinkle over the herbs.

4 Pour over the garlic butter and season well.

5 Fold the foil over to make a well sealed parcel.

6 Place the package on a baking sheet and place in the oven for 30 minutes or until the potatoes are soft.

Serves: 4

Preparation time: 15 minutes

Salads & Sides by Meriel Bradley :: www.MerielBradley.com

New Potatoes in Garlic Parsley Butter

1½ pounds small new potatoes
1 cup chopped fresh parsley
4 tablespoons butter melted with 1 clove of crushed garlic
Fresh ground salt and pepper to taste

1 Wash all vegetable ingredients well before chopping.

2 Pre-heat the oven to 375 degrees F.

3 Lay the potatoes on a large piece of foil and sprinkle over the parsley.

4 Pour over the garlic butter and season well.

5 Fold the foil over to make a well sealed parcel.

6 Place the package on a baking sheet and place in the oven for 45 minutes or until the potatoes are soft.

Serves: 4 - 5

Preparation time: 15 minutes

Sweet Potatoes Roasted with Lemon

1 pound sweet potatoes
     peeled and cut into pieces
     2 inches square
2 tablespoons olive oil
1 lemon
1 tablespoon chopped fresh
     thyme
Fresh ground salt and pepper
     to taste

1. Wash all vegetable ingredients well before chopping.

2. Pre-heat oven to 375 degrees F.

3. Place the sweet potatoes in a roasting pan and pour over the olive oil.

4. Turn the potatoes over to coat in the oil.

5. Zest or grate the rind from the lemon and sprinkle over the potatoes.

6. Sprinkle over the thyme and season well.

7. Cook for 30 minutes or until tender turning once or twice during cooking.

Serves: 2

Preparation time: 10 minutes

Salads & Sides by Meriel Bradley :: www.MerielBradley.com

Foil Baked
Sweet Potatoes

1 large sweet potato peeled
and cut into home fries
2 tablespoons red wine
2 tablespoons honey
2 tablespoons olive oil
Fresh ground salt to taste

1 Wash the potatoes well before chopping.

2 Pre-heat oven to 375 degrees F.

3 Lay the potatoes on a large piece of foil and sprinkle over the salt.

4 Pour over the wine, honey and olive oil.

5 Fold the foil over to make a well sealed parcel.

6 Place the package on a baking sheet and place in the oven for 45 minutes or until the potatoes are soft.

Serves: 4

Preparation time: 10 minutes

Salt Baked Potatoes

4 baking potatoes
1 tablespoon fresh ground salt
Butter to taste

1 Pre-heat oven to 400 degrees F.

2 Scrub potatoes and roll in the salt while still wet and place on a baking sheet.

3 Cook for 60 minutes or until soft.

4 Using oven gloves cut a cross in the top of each potato. Squeeze the sides to open up the inside.

5 Serve with butter.

Serves: 4

Preparation time: 5 minutes

Salads & Sides by Meriel Bradley :: www.MerielBradley.com

Baked Potatoes Stuffed with Corn & Cheese

4 baking potatoes
1 tablespoon fresh ground salt
1 can corn
2 cups cheese grated
Butter to taste

1 Pre-heat oven to 400 degrees F.

2 Scrub potatoes and roll in the salt while still wet and place on a baking sheet.

3 Cook for 60 minutes or until soft.

4 Heat the corn.

5 Using oven gloves cut a cross in the top of each potato. Squeeze the sides to open up the inside.

6 To each potato, add the butter, spoon over the corn and top with the cheese.

Serves: 4

Preparation time: 10 minutes

Baked Potato Stuffed with Cheese & Onion

4 baking potatoes
1 tablespoon fresh ground salt
1 medium onion diced
1 tablespoon butter
2 cups cheese grated
Butter to taste

1 Pre-heat oven to 400 degrees F.

2 Scrub potatoes and roll in the salt while still wet and place on a baking sheet.

3 Cook for 60 minutes or until soft.

4 Melt 1 tablespoon butter in a pan and saute the onion until soft.

5 Using oven gloves cut a cross in the top of each potato. Squeeze the sides to open up the inside.

6 To each potato, add the butter, spoon over the onion and top with the cheese.

Serves: 4

Preparation time: 10 minutes

Salads & Sides by Meriel Bradley :: www.MerielBradley.com

Potato Stuffed with Cheese & Tuna

4 baking potatoes
1 tablespoon fresh ground salt
1 can tuna drained
1 tablespoon butter
2 cups cheese grated
Butter to taste

1 Pre-heat oven to 400 degrees F.

2 Scrub potatoes and roll in the salt while still wet.

3 Cook for 60 minutes or until soft.

4 Allow to cool, then cut the potatoes into halves and scoop out the insides from the skin.

5 Place the scooped out potato in a bowl and add the tuna and cheese.

6 Mix well.

7 Refill the potato skins with the potato, tuna and cheese mix and add a little butter to the top of each half.

8 Place on a baking try and put the potato halves back into the oven for 15 minutes.

Serves: 4

Preparation time: 15 minutes

Spicy Potato Wedges

6 large yellow flesh potatoes
6 tablespoons olive oil
3 teaspoons fresh ground
    pepper
Fresh ground salt to taste

1 Wash the potatoes well.

2 Place potatoes in a pan of cold water, bring to a boil and cook for 10 minutes.

3 Pre-heat oven to 400 degrees F.

4 Mix oil and pepper together.

5 Drain the potatoes and allow to cool.

6 Cut each potato in half and then each half into 4 wedges.

7 Roll the wedges in the oil /pepper mix and spread out onto a baking tray.

8 Cook for 20 - 30 minutes or until crisp.

Serves: 4

Preparation time: 15 minutes

Potatoes & Mushrooms with fresh Herbs

6 Yukon gold or yellow fleshed
   potato thinly sliced
1 pound white mushrooms
   sliced
2 tablespoons butter
1 tablespoon olive oil
2 tablespoons chopped fresh
   basil
1 tablespoon chopped fresh
   thyme
6 tablespoons chopped fresh
   parsley

> **QUICK TIP**
> *Parsley is rich in iron, vitamin
> A and vitamin C. Often used
> in stuffings, soups, sauces
> and many other dishes.*

1 Wash all vegetable ingredients well before chopping.

2 Pre-heat oven to 400 degrees F.

3 Melt 1 tablespoon of butter with the olive oil in a skillet
and saute the mushrooms until soft.

4 Grease a 9 x13 inch ovenproof dish and layer with $1/3$ of
the potatoes. Season with salt and fresh ground pepper to
taste. Layer on $1/3$ of the mushrooms and $1/3$ of the herbs.

5 Repeat layering twice and then dot the top with the
remaining butter.

6 Cover and bake for about 40 minutes or until the potatoes
are soft.

Serves: 4 - 6

Preparation time: 15 minutes

Bread

Corn Bread

1 cup cornmeal
1 cup whole wheat flour
$1/3$ cup sugar
4 teaspoons baking powder
$1/2$ teaspoon salt
1 cup buttermilk
1 beaten egg
5 tablespoons melted butter

1 Pre-heat oven to 375 degrees F.

2 Mix dry ingredients together.

3 Stir in buttermilk, butter and the beaten egg.

4 Mix gently.

5 Pour into a greased 9 inch square baking pan.

6 Bake for 30 minutes or until a toothpick comes out clean when inserted in the centre.

7 Cool slightly and cut into squares.

Serves: 6 - 8

Preparation time: 15 minutes

Salads & Sides by Meriel Bradley :: www.MerielBradley.com

Garlic Bread Loaf

6 tablespoons soft butter
2 cloves garlic crushed to a
   paste with 1/4 teaspoon
   salt
2 teaspoons dried parsley
1 French stick loaf

1 Pre-heat oven to 400 degrees F.

2 Blend the butter, garlic paste, and parsley together.

3 Make slits, as if cutting a slice, along the French stick, at regular intervals. Be careful not to cut all the way through.

4 Press the sides of the loaf to open the slits.

5 Spread the slits with the garlic butter.

6 Put on a baking try and into the oven for 10 minutes or until heated through.

Serves: 4 - 6

Preparation time: 10 minutes

Garlic Bread with Cheese

6 tablespoons soft butter
2 cloves garlic crushed to a
    paste with $1/4$ teaspoon salt
2 teaspoons dried parsley
1 French stick loaf
1 cup grated Mozzarella cheese
1 cup grated sharp cheddar
    cheese

1. Pre-heat oven to 400 degrees F.

2. Blend the butter, garlic paste, and parsley together.

3. Cut slices along the length of the French stick and lay them on a baking tray.

4. Spread the slices with the garlic butter and sprinkle with the cheeses.

5. Put the baking tray into the oven for 10 minutes or until heated through and the cheese has melted.

Serves: 4 - 6

Preparation time: 10 minutes

Salads & Sides by Meriel Bradley :: www.MerielBradley.com

Scones

Cheese Scones

2 cups flour
4 teaspoons baking powder
$\frac{1}{8}$ teaspoon salt
$\frac{1}{8}$ teaspoon celery salt
$\frac{1}{8}$ teaspoon mustard powder
4 tablespoons butter
1 cup finely grated cheese
Milk to mix

1 Pre-heat oven to 400 degrees F.

2 Mix the dry ingredients together.

3 Add the butter and rub in.

4 Mix in the cheese.

5 Mix to a soft rolling consistency with the milk.

6 Roll to $\frac{1}{2}$ an inch thick and cut into desired shapes.

7 Cook for 10 minutes or until firm to the touch.

QUICK TIP
When preparing scones, try to handle the dough as little as possible. The more you work with it the tougher your scones will be.

Serves: 4 - 6

Preparation time: 15 minutes

Salads & Sides by Meriel Bradley :: www.MerielBradley.com

Herb Scones

2 cups flour
4 teaspoons baking powder
$1/8$ teaspoon salt
$1/8$ teaspoon celery salt
$1/8$ teaspoon mustard powder
4 tablespoons butter
2 teaspoons dried Italian
    seasoning
Milk to mix

1. Pre-heat oven to 400 degrees F.

2. Mix the dry ingredients together.

3. Add the butter and rub in.

4. Mix in the herbs.

5. Mix to a soft rolling consistency with the milk.

6. Roll to $1/2$ an inch thick and cut into desired shapes.

7. Cook for 10 minutes or until firm to the touch.

Serves: 4 - 6

Preparation time: 15 minutes

Ham & Onion Scones

2 cups flour
4 teaspoons baking powder
$^1/_8$ teaspoon salt
$^1/_8$ teaspoon celery salt
$^1/_8$ teaspoon mustard powder
4 tablespoons butter
$^1/_2$ cup chopped ham
$^1/_2$ small onion very finely
diced
2 teaspoons dried Italian
seasoning
Milk to mix

1. Pre-heat oven to 400 degrees F.

2. Mix the dry ingredients together.

3. Add the butter and rub in.

4. Mix in the ham, onion and herbs.

5. Mix to a soft rolling consistency with the milk.

6. Roll to $^1/_2$ an inch thick and cut into desired shapes.

7. Cook for 10 minutes or until firm to the touch.

Serves: 4 - 6

Preparation time: 15 minutes

Pasta

Pasta with Toasted Pine Nuts & Sun Dried Tomatoes

4 cups cooked pasta well
    drained
2 tablespoons olive oil
2 cloves garlic crushed
2 green onions chopped
6 sun dried tomatoes chopped
$^1/_2$ tablespoon dried Italian
    seasoning
4 cups baby spinach
$^1/_3$ cup grated parmesan cheese
$^1/_3$ cup toasted pine nuts
Fresh ground salt and pepper
    to taste

1 Heat the oil in a pan and add garlic and green onions.

2 Saute on a low heat until soft.

3 Add tomatoes and herbs and saute for 1 minute.

4 Mix in the cooked pasta and spinach.

5 Season well and toss the pasta until all ingredients are heated through. Transfer to a serving dish.

6 Top with the parmesan cheese and pine nuts and serve.

Serves: 2 - 4

Preparation time: 15 minutes

Salads & Sides by Meriel Bradley :: www.MerielBradley.com

Pasta with Tomatoes & Mushrooms

4 cups cooked pasta well
   drained
2 tablespoons olive oil
1 medium onion chopped
2 cloves garlic crushed
1 1/2 cups mushrooms sliced
2 cups diced tomatoes
1/2 tablespoon dried oregano
Fresh ground salt and pepper
   to taste

1   Heat the oil in a pan and add the garlic and onion.

2   Saute until soft.

3   Add the mushrooms and herbs and saute for 1 minute.

4   Mix in the tomatoes and cook for 5 minutes.

5   Season well and add the cooked pasta.

6   Toss the pasta until all the ingredients are heated through.

Serves: 2 - 4

Preparation time: 15 minutes

Herb Garlic Pasta

4 cups cooked pasta well
    drained
2 cloves garlic crushed to a
    paste with $1/4$ teaspoon salt
1 tablespoon olive oil
1 cup chopped fresh parsley
$1/4$ cup chopped fresh basil
1 tablespoon chopped fresh
    thyme
$1/4$ cup toasted pine nuts
$1/4$ cup grated parmesan cheese
Fresh ground salt and pepper
    to taste

QUICK TIP

*There are many different
varieties of basil available.
It is often used in tomato
based dishes and pesto sauce.*

1. Heat the oil gently in a pan and add the garlic.

2. Saute for 1 minute.

3. Add the herbs and mix.

4. Season well and add the pasta.

5. Toss the cooked pasta until heated through. Transfer to a serving dish.

6. Top with the parmesan cheese and pine nuts and serve.

Serves: 2 - 4

Preparation time: 10 minutes

Salads & Sides by Meriel Bradley :: www.MerielBradley.com

Spaghetti with Garlic Oil

4 cups cooked spaghetti well
   drained
6 cloves garlic
4 tablespoons olive oil
1 cup finely chopped fresh
   parsley
$^1/_3$ cup Parmesan cheese

1 Peel the garlic cloves and crush slightly with the flat blade of a knife.

2 Heat the oil and add the garlic.

3 Cook gently until the garlic has turned brown.

4 Remove the garlic and add the cooked spaghetti and parsley.

5 Toss the pasta until heated through. Transfer to a serving dish.

6 Top with the parmesan cheese and serve.

Serves: 2 - 4

Preparation time: 10 minutes

Rice

Lemon Rice

4 cups cooked rice well
    drained
1 teaspoon black mustard
    seeds
$^1/_2$ tablespoon oil
1 tablespoon shredded
    coconut
Juice and zest 1 lemon
$^1/_2$ cup chopped fresh cilantro

1 Place the oil and mustard seeds in a pan and gently heat until the mustard seeds start to pop.

2 Add the cooked rice and heat through.

3 Add the coconut, lemon juice and zest and the cilantro.

4 Mix well.

Serves: 2 - 4

Preparation time: 10 minutes

Salads & Sides by Meriel Bradley :: www.MerielBradley.com

Garlic Parsley Rice

4 cups cooked rice well
    drained
2 tablespoons butter
1 clove garlic crushed to a
    paste with $1/4$ teaspoon
    salt
1 cup chopped fresh parsley

1 Melt the butter in a pan and add the garlic paste.

2 Cook for 4 minutes and add the parsley and cooked rice.

3 Mix well and heat through.

Serves: 2 - 4

Preparation time: 10 minutes

Rice with Fruit & Nuts

4 cups cooked rice well
   drained
1 medium onion diced
½ tablespoon butter
2 tablespoons raisins
2 tablespoons toasted pine nuts
2 tablespoons toasted almonds
2 tablespoons chopped fresh
   cilantro

1. Melt the butter and gently cook the onion until soft.

2. Add the raisins and cook for 1 minute.

3. Add the cooked rice and heat through.

4. Stir in the nuts and cilantro and serve immediately.

QUICK TIP

*To roast nuts, dry roast them
in a frying pan. Do not add
oil to the pan. Use a gentle
heat and keep moving the
nuts around the pan with a
spoon for even browning.*

Serves: 2 - 4

Preparation time: 10 minutes

Coconut Rice

1 cup basmati rice
2¼ cups coconut milk
1 teaspoon salt

1 Wash the rice and place in a pan with the coconut milk.

2 Cook for ten minutes stirring often.

3 Add the salt.

4 Cover and bring to the boil.

5 Reduce the heat and cook gently until the coconut milk is absorbed and the rice is tender, making sure the rice does not stick to the bottom of the pot.

Serves: 1 - 2

Preparation time: 10 minutes

Rice with Corn & Peas

4 cups cooked rice well
    drained
1 medium onion diced
$1/2$ tablespoon butter
2 cups frozen peas
2 cups frozen corn

1 Heat the butter in a pan and add the onion.

2 Cook until soft.

3 Add the peas and corn and cook for 3 minutes.

4 Add the cooked rice, mix well, and heat through.

Serves: 2 - 4

Preparation time: 10 minutes

Salads & Sides by Meriel Bradley :: www.MerielBradley.com

Yellow Rice with Almonds & Coconut

4 cups cooked rice well
  drained
1 tablespoon butter
2 whole cardamoms
2 whole cloves
1 stick cinnamon
1 teaspoon turmeric powder
1 tablespoon ground almonds
1 tablespoon shredded
  coconut

1 Melt the butter and add the cardamoms, cloves and cinnamon stick.

2 Cook for 2 minutes.

3 Add the cooked rice, turmeric, almonds and coconut.

4 Remove the cardamoms, cloves and cinnamon stick before serving if possible.

Serves: 2 - 4

Preparation time: 10 minutes

Vegetables

Carrots with Cumin Seeds

8 large carrots peeled, ends removed and cut into strips
2 teaspoons cumin seeds
1 tablespoon butter
Fresh ground salt to taste

1 Wash the carrots well and dry before chopping.

2 Steam or boil the carrots until just cooked.

3 Melt the butter in a pan and add the cumin seeds.

4 Cook the cumin seeds gently for a few minutes taking care not to burn the butter.

5 Add the cooked carrots and mix well.

6 Season to taste.

Serves: 4

Preparation time: 10 minutes

Salads & Sides by Meriel Bradley :: www.MerielBradley.com

Honey Glazed Carrots

12 medium carrots peeled
    with the ends removed
2 tablespoons butter
1 tablespoon soft brown sugar
1 pinch nutmeg
1 pinch cinnamon
2 tablespoons honey

1 Wash the carrots well and dry.

2 Pre-heat the oven to 375 degrees F.

3 Place the carrots on a piece of foil big enough to make a parcel with the carrots.

4 Dot over the butter, sprinkle over the sugar, cinnamon and nutmeg, and drizzle over the honey.

5 Make a parcel with the foil and place on a baking tray.

6 Cook for 30 - 40 minutes or until the carrots have reached desired tenderness.

Serves: 4

Preparation time: 10 minutes

Carrots with Nuts & Peas

1 pound carrots peeled and
    cut into strips
2 tablespoons oil
1 medium onion sliced
1 tablespoon mustard seeds
1 cup chicken stock
2 tomatoes diced
½ teaspoon ground
    powdered ginger
2 cups frozen peas
1 cup toasted cashew nuts

1. Wash the carrots well and dry before chopping.

2. Heat the oil in a pan and add the onion and mustard seeds.

3. Saute gently until the onion is soft.

4. Add the chicken stock and carrots.

5. Cover and cook the carrots until just tender, adding more stock if necessary.

6. Add the tomatoes, ginger and peas and heat through.

7. Simmer to thicken the sauce if it is too watery.

8. Stir in the cashews just before serving.

Serves: 4

Preparation time: 15 minutes

Salads & Sides by Meriel Bradley :: www.MerielBradley.com

Mushroom & Bean Sprout Stir Fry

2 green onions chopped
1 tablespoon oil
2 cups sliced mushrooms
1 tablespoon soy sauce
1 cup baby corn sliced
2 cups bean sprouts

1. Wash all vegetables well and dry before chopping.

2. Heat the oil in a pan and add the green onions.

3. Saute for 2 minutes.

4. Add the mushrooms and soy sauce and saute for 3 minutes.

5. Add the baby corn and bean sprouts and saute for 2 minutes.

Serves: 2 - 4

Preparation time: 10 minutes

Garlic Portobello Mushrooms

4 large Portobello mushrooms
4 cloves garlic diced
2 tablespoons soft butter
Fresh ground salt and pepper
    to taste

1 Pre-heat the oven to 400 degrees F.

2 Remove and chop the stalks of the washed mushrooms.

3 Mix the chopped stalks with the butter, garlic and black pepper.

4 Place each mushroom on a piece of foil.

5 Divide the garlic butter mix between the mushrooms and spread on top.

6 Wrap the foil around each mushroom and place on a baking tray.

7 Cook for 10 minutes or until mushrooms reach desired tenderness.

Serves: 2 - 4

Preparation time: 10 minutes

Mushrooms with Herbs

4 cups mushrooms sliced
1 tablespoon butter
1 medium onion finely diced
1 clove garlic diced
1 teaspoon dried thyme
1 teaspoon dried summer
   savory
$1/3$ cup chopped fresh parsley
Fresh ground salt and
   pepper to taste

1 Wash all vegetables well and dry before chopping.

2 Melt the butter in a pan and add the onion and garlic.

3 Saute for 2 minutes.

4 Add the dried herbs and the mushrooms.

5 Mix well. Saute for 2 minutes.

6 Season well and add the parsley.

7 Cook for 2 more minutes or until desired tenderness is reached.

QUICK TIP

Pick savory leaves before the flowers appear. This herb has a subtle flavor good for a wide variety of dishes.

Serves: 2 - 4

Preparation time: 10 minutes

Garlic Snow Peas

1 pound snow peas ends
    removed
2 cloves garlic crushed with
    $1/4$ teaspoon salt
1 teaspoon brown sugar
1 tablespoon butter

1. Wash the snow peas and dry.

2. Melt the butter in a pan and add the garlic paste and sugar.

3. Saute gently for 1 minute.

4. Add the snow peas and saute for 3 minutes or until desired tenderness is reached.

Serves: 2 - 4

Preparation time: 10 minutes

Salads & Sides by Meriel Bradley :: www.MerielBradley.com

Stuffed Peppers

2 peppers seeded, cored, and
    cut in half
1 cup cooked rice
1 small onion chopped
1 clove of garlic chopped
$^1/_2$ cup salsa
$^1/_2$ cup chopped fresh parsley
6 mushrooms chopped
Fresh ground salt and pepper
    to taste

1. Wash all vegetables well and dry before chopping.

2. Mix all the ingredients except the peppers together and season well.

3. Spoon the stuffing mix into the pepper halves and place on a baking sheet.

4. Cook at 375 degrees F. for 45 minutes or until filling is heated through. Cover with foil if the top starts to over brown.

Serves: 2 - 4

Preparation time: 15 minutes

Baked Eggplant & Tomatoes

1 tablespoon oil
1 Spanish onion sliced
2 cloves garlic chopped
1 teaspoon ground coriander
1 teaspoon ground cumin
1 teaspoon paprika
2 eggplants cut into 1 inch
 strips
4 tablespoons tomato paste
1 large tin diced tomatoes
 (approx. 28 fl. oz.)
Fresh ground salt to taste

QUICK TIP

Cilantro looks very similar to plain leaf parsley, but its flavor is very different. It is most often used in Indian cooking.

1. Wash all vegetables well and dry before chopping.

2. Pre-heat the oven to 375 degrees F.

3. Heat the oil in a pan and add the onion and garlic.

4. Saute for 3 minutes and add the coriander, cumin and paprika plus 2 tablespoons tomato juice from the diced tomatoes.

5. Saute for 2 more minutes and add the tomatoes and tomato paste.

6. Add the eggplant, mix well and heat through.

7. Transfer into a baking dish and cover.

8. Cook in the oven for 40 - 50 minutes or until the eggplant is done.

Serves: 2 - 4

Preparation time: 15 minutes

Salads & Sides by Meriel Bradley :: www.MerielBradley.com

Eggplant Fritters

1 eggplant thinly sliced
1 cup milk
1 cup cornstarch (this might
    vary depending on the
    size of the eggplants)
Oil for frying
Fresh ground salt to taste

1 Wash the eggplant well and dry before chopping.

2 Place the eggplant slices in the milk and leave for 2 minutes.

3 Heat $^3/_4$ inch of oil in a frying pan.

4 Dip each slice of egg plant into the cornstarch coating each side.

5 Shake off any excess and shallow fry the slices in batches until crisp.

6 Drain on triple folded paper towel.

7 Season to taste with salt and serve.

Serves: 2 - 4

Preparation time: 10 minutes

Spiced Zucchini

4 zucchini sliced in circles
   $1/2$ inch thick
2 tablespoons oil
1 medium onion diced
$1/4$ teaspoon chili powder
$1/4$ teaspoon mustard seeds
$1/4$ teaspoon coriander seeds
$1/4$ teaspoon cumin seeds
Fresh ground salt to taste

1 Wash zucchini well and dry before chopping.

2 Heat 1 tablespoon oil in a pan and add the zucchini.

3 Saute for 2 minutes and remove to a bowl.

4 Add the remaining oil to the pan and saute the onion until soft.

5 Add all the spices and seasonings and saute for 3 more minutes.

6 Return the zucchini to the pan and continue cooking for 2 - 3 minutes or until desired tenderness is reached.

Serves: 2 - 4

Preparation time: 15 minutes

Salads & Sides by Meriel Bradley :: www.MerielBradley.com

Ratatouille

3 zucchini sliced
2 tablespoons olive oil
1 onion diced
2 cloves garlic chopped
1/2 pound green beans sliced
1 large tin diced tomatoes
   (approx. 28 fl. oz.)
4 tablespoons tomato paste
1 1/2 cups mushrooms sliced
1 tablespoon oregano
Fresh ground salt and pepper
   to taste

1 Wash all vegetables well and dry before chopping.

2 In a large pan heat the oil and saute the onion until soft.

3 Add the garlic and saute for 1 minute.

4 Add the zucchini and green beans and saute for 10 minutes.

5 Add the tomatoes, tomato paste, mushrooms, oregano and season to taste.

6 Cover the pan and cook slowly for 45 - 60 minutes.

QUICK TIP

Oregano has multiple uses in the kitchen – it has a mild peppery flavor which is great for soups and sauces.

Serves: 4 - 6

Preparation time: 15 minutes

Herby Green Beans with Carrots & Peppers

1 pound green beans ends
   removed
1 tablespoon olive oil
1 medium onion diced
2 cloves garlic diced
4 large carrots peeled and
   cut into strips about the
   size of the beans
4 tomatoes diced
1 red pepper seeded and diced
1 tablespoon chopped fresh
   thyme
1 tablespoon chopped fresh
   oregano
Fresh ground salt and pepper
   to taste

1 Wash all vegetables well and dry before chopping.

2 Place the olive oil in a pan and saute the onion and garlic for 3 minutes.

3 Add the remaining ingredients and cook with the lid on the pan, stirring occasionally, for 15 minutes or until the beans and carrots reach the desired tenderness.

4 Add a little water or tomato juice if it becomes too dry.

Serves: 4

Preparation time: 15 minutes

Green Beans & Tomatoes

1 pound green beans ends
    removed
1 tablespoon olive oil
1 clove garlic
1 onion sliced
2 tomatoes diced
$1/2$ cup parsley
$1/2$ teaspoon French mustard
$1/2$ teaspoon salt
2 tablespoons tomato puree
$1/3$ cup water

1. Wash all vegetables well and dry before chopping.

2. Heat the olive oil in a pan and saute the onion and garlic until golden.

3. Add the beans and $1/2$ the water and cover.

4. Cook gently for 10 minutes.

5. Blend the other $1/2$ of the water and tomato paste until smooth.

6. Add the diced tomatoes, tomato paste mixture, and seasonings to the pan.

7. Cook until the beans reach desired tenderness.

8. Add a little water or tomato juice if it becomes too dry.

Serves: 2 - 4

Preparation time: 10 minutes

Green Beans & Ginger

1 pound green beans, ends
   removed, steamed or
   boiled until just tender
1 tablespoon butter
1 medium onion diced
1 clove garlic diced
1 tablespoon grated fresh
   peeled ginger root
Fresh ground salt to taste

1 Melt the butter in a pan and add the onion, garlic and ginger.

2 Saute until soft.

3 Add the beans and salt and heat through.

Serves: 4

Preparation time: 10 minutes

Salads & Sides by Meriel Bradley :: www.MerielBradley.com

Foil Baked Leeks with Lime

4 leeks tops and roots
    trimmed away, sliced in
    $1/2$ along the length and
    washed well, trying to
    keep each $1/2$ in one piece
2 cloves garlic crushed
Juice of 2 limes
2 teaspoons sugar
1 tablespoon olive oil
2 sprigs fresh rosemary
Fresh ground salt & pepper
    to taste

QUICK TIP

Rosemary is a very aromatic herb with a unique flavor. It is often used to complement chicken and lamb.

1. Wash all vegetables well and dry before chopping.

2. Pre-heat the oven to 375 degrees F.

3. Mix the garlic, lime juice, sugar and olive oil together.

4. Lay the leeks on a large piece of foil and place the rosemary sprigs in between.

5. Pour over the garlic and lime juice mix and season with pepper to taste.

6. Fold the foil over to make a well sealed parcel.

7. Place the package on a baking sheet and place in the oven for 30 minutes or until the leeks are soft.

Serves: 4

Preparation time: 10 minutes

Foil Baked Leeks with Tomatoes & Potatoes

4 leeks tops and roots
  trimmed away and sliced
  (be sure to wash leeks
  very well)
4 tomatoes diced
4 yellow flesh potatoes diced
3 tablespoons olive oil
2 cloves garlic crushed
1 teaspoon celery salt
Fresh ground pepper to taste

1. Wash all vegetables well and dry before chopping.

2. Pre-heat the oven to 375 degrees F.

3. Mix the garlic and olive oil together

4. Lay the leeks, potatoes and tomatoes on a large piece of foil.

5. Pour over the garlic olive oil and season with the celery salt and pepper to taste.

6. Fold the foil over to make a well sealed parcel.

7. Place the package on a baking sheet and place in the oven for 30 minutes or until the leeks and potatoes are soft.

Serves: 4

Preparation time: 15 minutes

Salads & Sides by Meriel Bradley :: www.MerielBradley.com

Roasted Pearl Onions & Parisian Potatoes with Garlic

1 pound Parisian potatoes
1 pound pearl onions peeled
8 cloves garlic halved
2 tablespoons butter melted
2 tablespoons olive oil
Fresh ground salt and pepper
    to taste

1. Wash the potatoes well and dry.

2. Pre-heat the oven to 375 degrees F.

3. In a large bowl, mix the butter, olive oil and seasonings together.

4. Add the potatoes, onions and garlic, and mix well.

5. Pour the contents of the bowl onto a baking tray.

6. Cook for 30 - 45 minutes or until the potatoes and onions are soft.

Serves: 4

Preparation time: 15 minutes

Onion Rings

1 large Spanish onion sliced
  into rings (spread on a
  paper towel to dry)
1 1/2 cups chickpea flour
  (available in health food
  stores)
1/2 cup milk
Oil for frying

1 Mix the flour and milk together to make a thick batter.

2 Allow to stand for 1/2 an hour to thicken.

3 Heat enough oil in a frying pan for shallow frying.
(Use a deep fat fryer - if you have one - following the
manufacturers instructions)

4 Add the onion rings to the batter coating them evenly.

5 Add the rings one batch at a time (1 layer of rings in the
frying pan) to the oil and fry until crisp on both sides.

6 Drain on triple folded paper towels.

Serves: 4

Preparation time: 15 minutes

Salads & Sides by Meriel Bradley :: www.MerielBradley.com

Herb Roast Onions

4 onions peeled
4 sprigs of rosemary
Fresh ground salt to taste

1 Pre-heat the oven to 350 degrees F.

2 Cut a cross in the top of each onion and turn the knife to make a small hole.

3 Insert the rosemary sprigs and sprinkle with the salt.

4 Place on a baking tray and cook for 35 - 40 minutes or until the onions are tender.

Serves: 4

Preparation time: 10 minutes

Cinnamon Roast Onions

4 onions peeled
4 cinnamon sticks
1 tablespoon sugar

1. Pre-heat the oven to 350 degrees F.

2. Cut a cross in the top of each onion and turn the knife to make a small hole.

3. Insert the cinnamon sticks and sprinkle with the sugar.

4. Place on a baking tray and cook for 35 - 40 minutes or until the onions are tender.

Serves: 4

Preparation time: 10 minutes

Garlic Roast Onions

4 onions peeled
4 cloves garlic peeled
Celery salt to taste

1. Pre-heat the oven to 350 degrees F.

2. Cut a cross in the top of each onion and turn the knife to make a small hole.

3. Insert the garlic cloves and sprinkle with the celery salt.

4. Place on a baking tray and cook for 35 - 40 minutes or until the onions are tender.

Serves: 4

Preparation time: 10 minutes

Just Peas

2 cups frozen peas
1 tablespoon butter

1   Bring 4 cups of water to the boil and add the peas.

2   Bring back to the boil and turn down to simmer for 1 minute.

3   Drain immediately place in a bowl and add the butter to the top.

Serves: 4

Preparation time: 5 minutes

Spicy Cauliflower

1 cauliflower cut into florets
1 tablespoon oil
2 onions sliced
1 teaspoon mustard powder
1 teaspoon ground ginger
2 teaspoons ground coriander
2 cups tomato juice
Fresh ground salt to taste
(be careful - some tomato
juices are already salted)

1. Wash the cauliflower well and dry before chopping.

2. Heat the oil in a pan and add the onion.

3. Saute until soft.

4. Add the mustard, ginger, coriander and 2 tablespoons of the tomato juice, and saute for 3 minutes.

5. Add the cauliflower and the remaining tomato juice.

6. Mix well and cover.

7. Cook slowly for 15 - 20 minutes or until the cauliflower is tender, stirring occasionally adding more tomato juice if necessary.

Serves: 4

Preparation time: 15 minutes

Baked Cauliflower Cheese

1 cauliflower cut into florets
and steamed or boiled until
½ cooked and drained
1 cup milk
1½ tablespoons cornstarch
1 tablespoon Margarine or
butter - optional
2 cups grated old cheddar
cheese

1. Wash the cauliflower well and dry before chopping.

2. Pre-heat the oven to 375 degrees F.

3. In a pan, stir the cornstarch into the milk and add the butter.

4. Cook on a low heat stirring constantly until mixture thickens.

5. Continue stirring, and cook for 1 minute more.

6. Remove from the heat. Reserve 4 tablespoons of cheese and add remainder to the pot. Stir until the cheese has melted.

7. Grease an oven proof dish and put in the well drained 1/2 cooked cauliflower.

8. Pour over the cheese sauce and sprinkle the top with the reserved cheese.

9. Cook for 25 - 30 minutes or until the cauliflower reaches desired tenderness.

Serves: 4 - 6

Preparation time: 15 minutes

Cauliflower with Corn Sauce

1 cauliflower cut into florets
   and steamed or boiled until
   $1/2$ cooked and drained
1 tablespoon butter
1 onion diced
$1 1/2$ cups corn
1 cup yogurt
Fresh ground salt to taste
Paprika for the top

1. Wash the cauliflower well and dry before chopping.

2. Pre-heat the oven to 375 degrees F.

3. In a pan melt the butter and saute the onion until soft.

4. Add the corn and cook for 3 minutes more.

5. Puree the corn and onion and add the yogurt mixing well.

6. Season to taste.

7. Grease an oven proof dish and put in the well drained $1/2$ cooked cauliflower.

8. Pour over the corn sauce, and sprinkle with paprika.

9. Cook for 25 - 30 minutes or until the cauliflower reaches its desired tenderness.

Serves: 4 - 6

Preparation time: 15 minutes

Spinach & Tomatoes

1 package frozen spinach
  defrosted, squeezed dry
  and chopped
1 tablespoon butter
1 onion diced
1 clove garlic crushed with
  ¼ teaspoon salt
1 teaspoon ground coriander
4 tomatoes diced

1 Wash the tomatoes well and dry before chopping.

2 Heat the butter in a pan and add the onion and garlic.

3 Saute until soft.

4 Add the coriander and saute for 3 minutes.

5 Add the spinach and tomatoes.

6 Mix well and cover.

7 Cook slowly for 10 minutes or until the spinach and tomatoes are cooked.

Serves: 4

Preparation time: 10 minutes

Salads & Sides by Meriel Bradley :: www.MerielBradley.com

Aromatic Swiss Chard

1 bundle of Swiss chard
2 cloves garlic chopped
1 tablespoon sesame oil
Fresh ground salt and pepper
    to taste

1 Wash the Swiss chard well and dry before chopping.

2 Strip the leaves from the central rib of the chard.

3 Chop the leaves and dice the rib. Keep them separated from each other.

4 Heat the oil and cook the garlic for 1 minute.

5 Add the diced ribs, put the lid on the pan, and cook until almost soft.

6 Add the leaves and season well.

7 Put the lid back on the pan and cook for 5 minutes stirring occasionally.

Serves: 4

Preparation time: 10 minutes

Baby Corn, Snow Peas & Water Chestnuts in Oyster Sauce

2 cups snow peas ends
   removed
1 tablespoon oil
1 onion sliced
1 can sliced water chestnuts
1 can baby corn sliced
$^2/_3$ cup oyster sauce

1 Wash the snow peas well.

2 Heat the oil and saute the onion until soft.

3 Add the snow peas and saute for 5 minutes more.

4 Add the baby corn, water chestnuts and oyster sauce.

5 Heat through and serve.

Serves: 4

Preparation time: 10 minutes

Salads & Sides by Meriel Bradley :: www.MerielBradley.com

Minted Stuffed Tomatoes

6 large tomatoes, tops removed, insides carefully scooped out and discarded

$1/4$ pound extra lean ground beef sauteed with 1 chopped onion and 2 cloves chopped garlic until cooked

1 cup cooked rice

1 cup canned diced tomatoes drained

2 tablespoons fresh mint leaves chopped

Celery salt to taste

Fresh ground black pepper to taste

1 Pre-heat the oven to 350 degrees F.

2 Mix all the ingredients together except the scooped out tomatoes and season to taste.

3 Salt the insides of the scooped out tomatoes, and fill with the stuffing mixture.

4 Place the tomatoes on a baking tray and cook for 35 - 40 minutes or until the tomatoes are soft.

QUICK TIP

Try turning your scooped out tomatoes upside down on some layers of paper towel to drain them if they are very juicy. This will help prevent splitting while cooking.

Serves: 4 - 6

Preparation time: 15 minutes

Tomatoes Stuffed with Spinach & Ricotta

6 large tomatoes, tops
  removed and insides
  carefully scooped out
  and discarded
$1/2$ tablespoon butter
1 onion diced
2 cloves garlic chopped
1 cup frozen spinach
  defrosted chopped and
  squeezed dry
1 cup ricotta cheese
1 cup chopped parsley
$1/2$ cup toasted pine nuts
1 tablespoon Italian
  seasoning
$1/2$ teaspoon nutmeg
Fresh ground salt and pepper
  to taste

1. Pre-heat the oven to 350 degrees F.

2. Melt the butter in a pan and saute the onion and garlic until soft.

3. Mix all the ingredients together except the scooped out tomatoes and season to taste.

4. Salt the insides of the scooped out tomatoes, and fill with the stuffing mixture.

5. Place the tomatoes on a baking tray and cook for 35 - 40 minutes or until the tomatoes are soft.

Serves: 4 - 6

Preparation time: 20 minutes

Salads & Sides by Meriel Bradley :: www.MerielBradley.com

Baked Zucchini Rolls

8 slices bread crusts
removed and flattened
with a rolling pin
1 zucchini sliced into thin
matchsticks
Butter for the bread
Celery salt and paprika to
taste

1. Pre-heat the oven to 375 degrees F.

2. Butter each slice of bread.

3. Season the buttered side with the celery salt and paprika.

4. On the unbuttered side of the bread, place a few pieces of zucchini at one end and roll up jelly roll style.

5. Place on a baking tray and cook for 10 - 15 minutes until the bread is golden.

Serves: 2 - 4

Preparation time: 10 minutes

Baked Green Onion Rolls

8 slices bread crusts
   removed and flattened
   with a rolling pin
4 scallions sliced into thin
   matchsticks
Butter for the bread
Celery salt and paprika
   to taste

1 Pre-heat the oven to 375 degrees F.

2 Butter each slice of bread.

3 Season the buttered side with the celery salt and paprika.

4 On the unbuttered side of the bread, place a few pieces of scallion at one end and roll up jelly roll style.

5 Place on a baking tray and cook for 10 - 15 minutes until the bread is golden.

Serves: 2 - 4

Preparation time: 10 minutes

Flavored Butters

Maple Mustard Butter

1 cup soft butter
1 tablespoon maple syrup
1 tablespoon Dijon style
    mustard

1 Blend the butter, maple syrup, and mustard together.

2 Cover and refrigerate until ready to use.

QUICK TIP

These butters are a great complement to freshly cooked vegetables. They can be prepared ahead of time to add that little something extra to your meal.

Makes: 1 cup

Preparation time: 10 minutes

Green Onion & Chive Butter

1 cup soft butter
1 tablespoon diced green
    onion
1 tablespoon chopped
    fresh chives

1 Wash all vegetables well and dry before chopping.

2 Blend the butter, green onion, and chives together.

3 Cover and refrigerate until ready to use.

Makes: 1 cup

Preparation time: 10 minutes

Garlic Lime Butter

1 cup soft butter
Zest of 1 lime
1 teaspoon lime juice
1 clove garlic crushed

1 Blend the butter, lime juice and zest, and garlic together.

2 Cover and refrigerate until ready to use.

Makes: 1 cup

Preparation time: 10 minutes

Salads & Sides by Meriel Bradley :: www.MerielBradley.com

Lemon Dill Butter

1 cup soft butter
1 tablespoon chopped
   fresh dill
Zest of 1 lemon
1 teaspoon lemon juice

1 Blend the butter, chopped dill, lemon juice and zest together.

2 Cover and refrigerate until ready to use.

Makes: 1 cup

Preparation time: 10 minutes

Lemon Butter

1 cup soft butter
Zest of 1 lemon
1 tablespoon lemon juice

1 Blend the butter, lemon juice and zest together.

2 Cover and refrigerate until ready to use.

Makes: 1 cup

Preparation time: 10 minutes

Herb Butter

1 cup soft butter
1 tablespoon chopped fresh
  parsley
1 teaspoon chopped fresh
  thyme
1 teaspoon chopped fresh
  oregano

1 Wash all herbs well and dry before chopping.

2 Blend the butter and herbs together.

3 Cover and refrigerate until ready to use.

Makes: 1 cup

Preparation time: 10 minutes

Garlic Parmesan Butter

1 cup soft butter
2 tablespoons parmesan cheese
1 tablespoon chopped fresh parsley
1 clove garlic crushed

① Blend the butter, parmesan cheese, parsley and garlic together.

② Cover and refrigerate until ready to use.

QUICK TIP

Having a party or get-together? Try offering several of these butters to your guests as well as plain butter. Use a melon baller to make decorative round spheres, or a potato peeler to make butter curls for that special finishing touch.

Makes: 1 cup

Preparation time: 10 minutes

Salads & Sides by Meriel Bradley :: www.MerielBradley.com

More
Meriel Bradley!

Please turn this page
for a bonus excerpt from

DESSERTS

the next volume in
Meriel Bradley's popular
cookbook series

Desserts

Banana Raisin Loaf

8 tablespoons butter
1 cup sugar
2 eggs
2 cups flour
2 teaspoons baking powder
1/2 teaspoon salt
1 teaspoon vanilla
2 large bananas mashed
1 cup raisins
Milk or buttermilk to mix

1. Pre-heat the oven to 350 degrees F.

2. Cream butter and sugar together until light and fluffy.

3. Add the eggs one at a time beating well after each addition.

4. Add the bananas and vanilla, mix in well.

5. Sift the dry ingredients together and fold into the banana mixture.

6. Add the raisins and fold in.

7. Add enough milk to form a mixture that will drop easily from a spoon.

8. Pour into a greased loaf pan and bake for 50 – 60 minutes or until a wooden pick inserted in the centre comes out clean.

Makes: 1 loaf

Preparation time: 20 minutes

Nutty Shortbread

1¼ cup soft butter
1¼ cups brown sugar
2 cups flour
1 tsp baking powder
½ tsp salt
1¼ cups chopped pecans

1 Pre-heat the oven to 350 degrees F.

2 Mix the butter and sugar together until creamy.

3 Add the dry ingredients and the nuts, and mix well.

4 Press the mixture into a greased 9 inch baking pan or a greased metal quiche dish.

5 Bake for 20 – 30 minutes until golden brown.

6 Cut into servings while still warm.

Makes: about 20 servings

Preparation time: 15 minutes

Desserts by Meriel Bradley :: www.MerielBradley.com

Strawberry Peach Crumble

Filling

1 1/2 cups strawberries halved
1 can peaches in juice
    (approx 14 oz)
2 tablespoons honey
1/8 teaspoon cinnamon

Topping

1/2 cup brown sugar
1/2 cup butter
1/2 cup coconut
1 1/4 cups flour

1. Drain the peaches and mix 1/2 cup of the juice with the honey and cinnamon.

2. Place the peaches and strawberries in a 9 inch pie dish and pour over the honey, cinnamon and juice mixture.

3. Pre-heat the oven to 325 degrees F.

4. In a bowl cream the sugar and butter together.

5. Add the flour a little at a time to make a crumbly mixture.

6. Mix in the coconut.

7. Sprinkle the mixture over the fruit in the pie dish.

8. Place in the oven and cook for 35 – 45 minutes until the fruit is bubbling and the top is golden.

9. Place foil over the top if it starts to over brown.

Serves: 4 - 6

Preparation time: 15 minutes

Index

Index by Page Number

POTATOES

BREAD

Index by Page Number

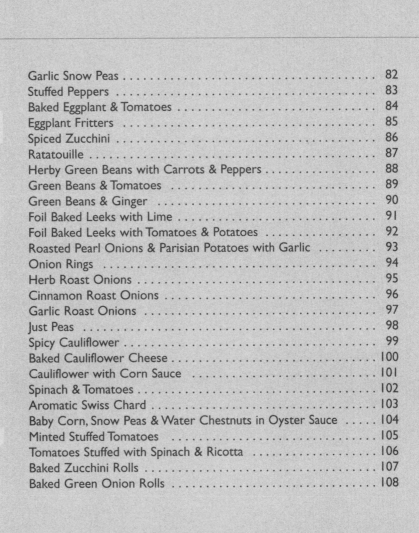

Index by Page Number

Thoughts, comments & new recipe ideas

Thoughts, comments & new recipe ideas

Jot down your thoughts, comments & new recipe ideas and send them to Meriel at:

meriel@merielbradley.com

Serves: _____

Preparation time: _____

Thoughts, comments & new recipe ideas

Serves: _____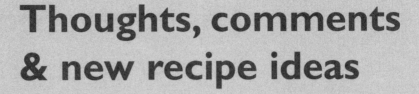

Preparation time: _____

Thoughts, comments & new recipe ideas

Jot down your thoughts, comments & new recipe ideas and send them to Meriel at:

meriel@merielbradley.com

Serves: _____

Preparation time: _____

Thoughts, comments & new recipe ideas

Serves: _____

Preparation time: _____

Thoughts, comments & new recipe ideas

Jot down your thoughts, comments & new recipe ideas and send them to Meriel at:

meriel@merielbradley.com

Serves: _____

Preparation time: _____

Thoughts, comments & new recipe ideas

Serves: _____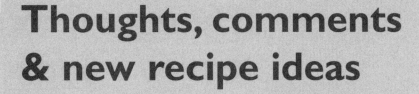

Preparation time: _____

Thoughts, comments & new recipe ideas

Jot down your thoughts, comments & new recipe ideas and send them to Meriel at:

meriel@merielbradley.com

Serves: _____

Preparation time: _____

Thoughts, comments & new recipe ideas

Serves: _____

Preparation time: _____

Thoughts, comments & new recipe ideas

Jot down your thoughts, comments & new recipe ideas and send them to Meriel at:

meriel@merielbradley.com

Serves: _____

Preparation time: _____